CLOTHES

PENNY MARSHALL

Macdonald

Jacket pictures

Front (main): Bargain hunters trying on hats, 1953
Front (small): The bridal party, 1895
Back (top): Lined up on the dance floor, 1927
Back (bottom): Rural workers, 1899

For Hannah, with love

A MACDONALD BOOK

First published in 1986 by
Macdonald & Co. (Publishers) Ltd
London and Sydney

© Macdonald & Co. (Publishers) Ltd 1986

ISBN 0 356 11395 7

Macdonald & Co. (Publishers) Ltd
Greater London House
Hampstead Road
London NW1 7QX

A BPCC PLC company

Printed by Purnell Book Production Ltd
Paulton, near Bristol, Avon

BRITISH LIBRARY CATALOGUING IN PUBLICATION DATA

Marshall, Penny
  Clothes.–(The Camera as witness; no. 9)
  1. Costume–Great Britain–
  History–19th century–
Juvenile literature
  2. Costume–Great Britain–
  History–20th century–
Juvenile literature
  I. Title   II. Series
  391'.0941   GT737

  ISBN 0-356-11395-7

CREDITS

Abbot Hall Art Gallery, Kendal: 4,
  9(bottom), 13(bottom)
Aberdeen City Libraries: 11, 19(top)
Barnaby's Picture Library: 40(top),
  42-43(top & bottom)
BBC Hulton Picture Library: back
  cover(top), 26-27, 27, 32(top &
  bottom), 38-39
Birmingham Central Library: front
  cover(inset), back cover(bottom),
  17(bottom), 20-21
Birmingham Post/Birmingham Central
  Library: 40-41
Bootle Library: 36(left)
Metropolitan Borough of Bury,
  Libraries and Arts Department:
  7(top right)
Edinburgh Library: 10(top right)
Greater London Photographic Library:
  22
Humberside County Council: 28(top)
Imperial War Museum: 25
Institute of Agricultural History/Mrs
  Iris Moon: 8, 10(top left), 14, 15
Leicestershire Museums, Art Galleries
  and Record Service: 17(top), 20,
  24(top)
Macdonald Library: 5, 34-35(bottom)
Margate Library, Local Studies
  Collection: 18-19
Motherwell District Council, Local
  Studies Library: 19(bottom)
National Library of Wales: 29
Northampton Museums: 16
Nottinghamshire County Library
  Service: 33
Borough of Poole, Museums Service:
  37
Humphrey Spender/Mass Observation
  Archive: 30, 31
John Topham Picture Library: front
  cover(main picture), 34-35(top),
  35(right), 38, 39(bottom), 43, 44
Vestry House Museum: 6, 9(top), 12,
  13(top), 23(top left & top right), 26,
  28(bottom), 30
Vestry House Museum/Waltham
  Forest Guardian: 36-37
Victoria and Albert Museum: 7(top left)

Picture research by Caroline Mitchell

Contents

Introduction

In 1850, when the photograph below was taken, Britain was a prosperous and powerful country. Queen Victoria had been on the throne for 13 years. Any initial fears, about the effects such a young monarch (she was only 18 when she became queen) might have on the country's stability, had long since been forgotten. At home the country was settled; abroad the British Empire was growing.

Looking back, the Victorian age can easily seem to be one long period of uninterrupted progress: the rich were certainly getting richer (and so were the growing middle classes); and although the poor were not getting richer, they weren't getting poorer either, as concerned social reformers worked hard to improve their lives.

The confidence of the country was reflected in the way people dressed. Women's clothes of the time, characterised by rich fabrics, opulent styles using a great deal of material, and decorations everywhere, were bulky and ornate.

Men, too, were very concerned about their appearance. A man could easily change his clothes three or four times a day: the Victorians considered it extremely important to wear exactly the right clothes for every occasion, which frequently meant that a different set of clothes was worn for breakfast, luncheon, tea and dinner.

But nothing is static, especially where clothes are concerned. Throughout the Victorian era, women particular were trying to change the restricting style of their clothes. This was generally accompanied by despairing complaints from their parents about 'the dreadful styles the young are adopting' – a familiar cry that has echoed down the ages.

The women out for a walk on page 13 would have been strongly condemned by the older lady on page 6, not only for their 'mannish' style of dress, but also for going for a walk 'striding about in such an unfeminine way'. Yet to us they seem quite demure.

As you can see from looking around you in the street, the trend for clothes in easier, freer styles continued. This reflects the far more informal way in which we now all live.

The informality today also marks another change in society: the breakdown of class barriers. In Victorian and Edwardian times, it was possible to tell someone's background immediately by the clothes they wore – though there were complaints that 'even factory girls want their bustles', meaning that they were getting ideas 'above their station' by wanting to copy the dress of their social superiors.

Today, countrywide chain stores, jeans and tee-shirts mean a uniformity of dress that would have horrified our predecessors 100 years ago.

Imagine, too, their shocked reaction to men and women wearing similar clothes, and ones that revealed so much bare flesh. Victorian attitudes can be summed up by a notice pinned up in the Wimbledon Croquet Club in 1870 which requested gentlemen 'not to play in their shirtsleeves when ladies are present'!

HOW TO USE THIS BOOK

The photos in this book give a good idea of the changes in clothes and the way people have dressed over the last century and a quarter. As you read through the book look out for the things that are different from today, and also for the things that are the same. You can tell, too, from people's expressions what they are thinking, and that certainly hasn't changed!

Learn to look closely at the photographs and to draw conclusions from what you see. Although many of them were never intended as such, all the photographs in this book are important documents in our social history.

The date at the top of each page tells you when the photograph was taken.

A NOTE ABOUT PHOTOGRAPHY

In the 1850s, when this book starts, photography was very much a new and unusual hobby, a pastime for a few scientifically-minded amateurs with servants to carry the heavy, cumbersome equipment. Taking photographs was a laborious process. The sitters had to stay absolutely still for several minutes while the image was exposed on the photographic plate. Any movement, however slight, would come out as a blur in the finished picture.

Early photographs were processed onto metal and glass as well as paper. Improvements came first through the experiments of individuals, usually working alone to solve problems. Early great pioneers included William Henry Fox Talbot, Frederick Scott Archer and the Frenchman, Louis Daguerre. Their discoveries made photography what it is today.

With today's cameras it is possible for anyone to take a photo – just point the camera and snap! But that hasn't reduced photography's important role as a recorder of history – the history of individuals as well as great events. Every photograph, however ordinary, can be considered an historical document. As you will discover in this book, there's a lot you can learn from a photograph!

The photograph below was taken in 1907. Cameras were already much simpler than in the very early days of photography, but were still slow and difficult to use.

(Left) Mr and Mrs Handley of Garside, in the Lake District, photographed in 1850. Notice the beautiful silk of which her dress is made, as well as her husband's striped trousers. Little ruffled white caps like hers were often worn by older women. The top hat on the left, resting upside down on the table (this made it much easier to pick up) has the tall wide crown, typical of top hats of the time.

1860

A FAMILY GROUP

This group, photographed in about 1860, gives a good idea of what prosperous middle-class Victorians were wearing.

Although having your picture taken was still quite an unusual event (photography was a very new discovery), these people don't appear to have 'dressed up' for the special occasion. The hat the girl on the right is holding on her knee may be for 'best', but the dress of the young woman on the left is just a plain, serviceable, everyday one.

Look at the enormous amount of material in these dresses. Apart from skirt lengths and the overall styles, this is probably the biggest contrast with our clothes today. Even if the dress materials themselves were plain, as these ones are, the sheer quantity of material makes the dresses seem extravagant.

And don't forget that, under them, the women would have been wearing layers of underclothes and petticoats, whose skirts would have been almost as full as the dresses. They would certainly keep them warm!

The men's clothes were not particularly comfortable, either, with those stiffly starched high collars cutting under the chin.

Whoever took this photograph was clearly quite skilful. Most of the group here seem relaxed and are smiling reasonably naturally. Today we take 'natural' photographs for granted, but when this group posed for a portrait some 125 years ago, they had to remain absolutely still for at least a minute, while the image registered on the specially-treated glass plate in the camera.

Looking relaxed for that long is harder than you might think: a happy smile soon becomes a silly smirk or disappears altogether. That's why the people in many old photographs appear so stiff and grim.

6

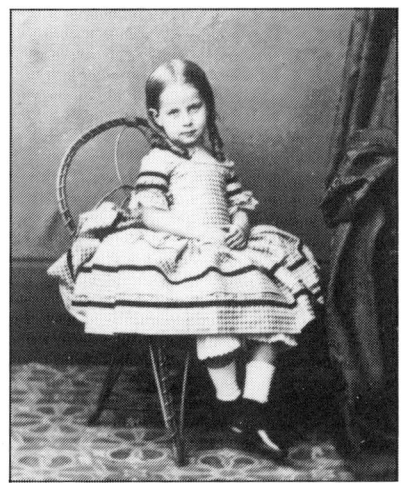

VIRGINIA GRACE

(Above) According to the name on the original photograph, this little girl is called Virginia Grace. She posed for her picture in November 1863, and obviously loved every minute of it.

She *is* dressed up for the occasion, from her neatly parted and ringletted hair to the tips of her little patent leather shoes. She's too small for her feet to rest on the carpet but, when you're the centre of attention, even that discomfort soon disappears!

As you can probably guess, she, too, comes from a comfortably-off middle-class family. It isn't her mother who twists the rags into Virginia's hair each night to make the ringlets, but a maid or nanny. And it is the same maid or nanny who dressed her for this special occasion, and on every other day, too.

Her checked dress is probably of silk taffeta, with dark velvet ribbons as trimming. The full skirt echoes the styles her mother and grown-up sisters wear, though of course their skirts come down to the ground. Like them, Virginia wears several layers of underclothes (despite the off-the-shoulder style of her dress, houses were very cold by our standards). You can see the bottoms of her pleated lace-trimmed pantaloons below the hem of her dress.

But there's one item in this picture which bridges the gap between Virginia's clothes and those of today. To judge from the wrinkles in her white socks, they fell down just as easily then as now!

HOUSEMAIDS

(Above) These four smartly dressed women are, in fact, servants. They worked as housemaids in the home of a prosperous Lancashire industrialist at the end of the 1860s.

These elaborate dresses were only for 'best', or for their afternoons off. Indoors, doing their work, they would probably have worn plainer clothes and some sort of uniform apron, perhaps with a frilled cap.

Notice the difference in the style of these dresses compared with those opposite. It's not because these ones are worn by servants, but because fashions had changed in the ten years or so that separate the two photographs. Each dress still uses a lot of material (look at all the pleats and tucking), but skirts are much less full. The bodices, too, are more closely fitting. And if you wonder how they all manage to have such small neat waists, the answer is simple – corsets.

Until at least the 1930s, every woman (except perhaps the very poorest) wore corsets from her late teens onwards. They were made of webbing, with whalebone for stiffening and to give them shape. As you look through the pages of this book, notice how women's shapes change. That, too, is due to corsets shaping the body to fit the latest fashion ideas.

1876

ON HOLIDAY

How would you like to have these as your holiday clothes – because that's what they are. The four children here were photographed in 1876, during a holiday at Llandudno in Wales.

Look carefully at all the detail in the photograph (the pale line running across from the hand of the boy on the left is the result of damage to the original print).

Both boys are wearing suits of thick tweed *and* bowler hats! The younger boy is also wearing a tweed waistcoat, and a shirt and tie. Across his waistcoat he carries a watch-chain (the watch is probably in the small pocket), just like his father.

If the children really are going for a scramble on the rocks and are not just posing for a special picture, the girls' hats are probably fixed in position with hat pins, as they're not tied under the chin. Hat pins were steel pins some 10 cm long, with one end pointed and the other ending in a decorative knob. You stuck the pointed end through the hat and into your hair. After a few scratches, you soon learned to avoid your head.

The children's boots are stout and definitely sensible, a far cry from today's trainers. But bowler hats hardly seem practical for a walk.

These clothes underline another difference between Victorian times and the present day. Children today are regarded as children, which is more surprising than you may think. For many centuries children were seen merely as miniature adults. That's why children's clothes were usually just small versions of the clothes their parents wore.

As you look through the book, you'll notice how this attitude has slowly changed, until today when children have their own fashions.

THE PRIZE-GIVING

(Above) There can be no doubt that these people really are dressed up. It's July 1887, and the day of the annual regatta. The races are over, and everyone has gathered for the prize-giving. You can see a large silver bowl in the centre of the table on which the prizes are displayed.

The photograph shows a wide variety of fashions, both men's and women's. But notice particularly the women in white on the left of the picture. They are all wearing dresses with bustles. In front, the skirt falls almost straight from waist to hem, but at the back is very full and supported by a special padded underskirt.

Notice, too, the large fringed shawl over the back of the chair on the right. Women usually wore shawls to keep warm out-of-doors since a coat large enough to wear over such full skirts would be a very awkward garment.

MOURNING DRESS

(Right) Today we find it difficult to talk about death and dying, especially if it affects those nearest us, but we are reasonably open about sex. With the Victorians, it was quite the reverse. Sex was an unmentionable subject; many women knew nothing about it until they married, and many men weren't much better informed either. Death, on the other hand, was a matter of general interest and frank discussion.

These two women are in deep mourning (that is, they are entirely dressed in black) which suggests they are mourning the death of a parent or of their husbands. There were degrees of mourning according to how closely related you were to the dead person, and how long it was since they had died. Some widows, notably Queen Victoria, remained in mourning for the rest of their lives. In general, however, two years' mourning was regarded as socially acceptable.

The Victorians loved jewellery, and being in mourning didn't stop them from wearing it. Special mourning jewellery was made in jet – because, of course, it is black. The woman on the right has a jet brooch pinned to the neck of her dress, and a chain of jet on her bodice. The other woman wears two heavy bracelets of carved jet.

A FARMING FAMILY

(Above) This man's proud of his family and happy to show it. He's probably a tenant farmer – working land rented from a large landowner. No working farmer's life was easy: there was none of today's modern machines, and farmers were even more at the mercy of the weather than now. Also, if a tenant farmer got behind with the rent, he could lose the farm – and with it his family's home and income.

This family looks quite confident and prosperous, even though the women appear to be in mourning. Perhaps the old lady's husband has died, or one of the family's children. Illnesses like mumps, measles and whooping cough were much more serious in Victorian times, and many children died from them each year.

Everyone in the group is dressed quite well, even though the man's clothes are far from new. The boy's suit, in particular, is very smart. He wears a straw boater, like the elder of his sisters.

The jacket of her little checked suit has velvet cuffs and trimming on the pockets, as well as the button-in velvet inset down the front. This is a clever way of ensuring that she (and any other child who wears it) doesn't grow out of the jacket too quickly: the buttons will be moved as she grows.

A CROFTER'S FAMILY

This, too, is a farming family, but what a contrast to the one on the left. These are crofters (small farmers) in the Highlands of Scotland, where the winters are longer, the summers shorter, and life harder, than anywhere else in the British Isles.

The family members are clearly in their working clothes, whereas those on the left are in their Sunday best. Their whole manner indicates how tough their lives are. Only the mother standing in the doorway in her jacket and long striped skirt looks at all cheerful. The old lady sitting on the doorstone, with her cap and tartan shawl, looks completely dejected and worn out by life.

Quite apart from the clothes, the homes which form the background to these two photographs, both taken in the 1890s, tell their own tale. The windows with their little gables, and the creepers growing up the walls (left), suggest a gentler climate than the stone-walled, heather-thatched single storey croft above.

Crofts had to withstand the snow and gales of Highland winters, so it was impractical to have many rooms or large windows (some crofts had no windows at all).

ABERDEEN FISH WOMEN

Surrounded by the evidence of their trade, these Aberdeen herring women pause for a few moments while their photograph is taken.

Today's fast film was not yet invented, and the image being photographed had to register on a specially treated glass plate in the camera. This could take at least a minute. If anyone moved during that time, they would appear in the photo as a blur.

The pause probably made a welcome break for these women, photographed in 1893. They spent their days surrounded by the stench of fish as they worked to gut the herrings brought in by the local fishing fleet.

Their rough appearance and rough clothes reflect the harshness of their lives.

Their arms and hands, swollen and calloused from working with the wet fish in all weathers, their hair and clothes reeking of fish, are a far cry even from the women in the picture on the left – and they, too, certainly knew what hard work was.

THREE CHILDREN

There are in fact two boys and one girl in this photograph, even though the boy on the right is wearing a skirt.

It was quite a common practice to dress boys in girls' clothes until they were about seven years old. In a poor family, this was generally because clothes had to last as long as possible and were handed down from one child to the next, regardless of whether the children were boys or girls. It was such a usual thing to do that at least the children wouldn't be teased because of it.

Sailor suits were popular for both boys and girls throughout most of the Victorian and Edwardian period. As you can see from these two suits, they weren't all identical. The decoration varied as did the tops, some of which were pulled on over the head, while others, generally the girls', had buttons down the front.

The lanyards, the specially knotted cords the boys are wearing tied around their necks, add an authentic nautical touch – lanyards were then part of a sailor's uniform.

The boys seem to be enjoying watching the photographer at work, while their sister looks less certain. Her white cotton pinafore is typical of girls' clothes of the time. In the days before washing machines and easy-care fabrics, a cotton pinafore, which was easy to wash, served the very practical purpose of keeping the dress beneath it clean.

Have a look at what the children are wearing on their feet. You'll see boots of one sort or another appearing in many of the pictures in this book.

THREE OLD PEOPLE

(Right) What a contrast these three old people make to the two women in the photograph above them. Their faces and clothes tell a tale of long, hard-working lives. For them, walking is a means of getting from one place to another. Probably the last time any of them took a leisurely stroll was while 'courting' – a good many years before they were photographed in this lane in 1898.

The long shapeless coat of the woman on the left has a little cape over the shoulders. Capes like this provided extra protection, and were often detachable. The coat looks rather badly made. Notice the uneven hemline, and the way the material puckers between the buttons.

The coat was probably home-made. Ready-made clothes were very slowly becoming more common among the middle classes, who lived within reach of large towns, but country people generally still had to make their own or, if they could afford it, go to a local dressmaker, whose skills varied greatly.

The other two old people are dressed much as working people in the country had dressed for generations. The old man's suit is not so very different in style from those of the boys on page 8. But the boys' suits are not patched at the knees, and are undoubtedly made of a much better quality cloth than the coarse material of this one.

STROLLING ALONG

These two young women are enjoying a gentle walk in Epping Forest, on the north-eastern outskirts of London, in 1897. They probably caught the horse-drawn omnibus (as the first buses were called) from their home in nearby Leytonstone, then a prosperous, leafy suburb.

If you compare their clothes with what you wear today to go for a country walk, you'll probably think they're ridiculously impractical. But look again at the ladies in white on page 9. That photograph was taken only ten years before this one, but notice how much more practical these clothes are.

The skirts may be long, but they're not made clumsy by a bustle at the back. And it's also possible to wear a jacket or coat over them – much more useful than a shawl if the weather turns chilly.

But, as usual, even this more sensible fashion has its extremes. Look at their sleeves. The woman on the right has 'leg of mutton' sleeves on her jacket, so-called because of their fullness at the shoulder and narrowness at the wrist. The other woman's sleeves are so full that she couldn't get a jacket over them anyway. So, despite the umbrellas, she'll be hoping for a dry day.

Notice how the woman on the left is wearing black leather gloves. The woman on the right is probably wearing gloves too, but in a paler colour. It was quite unheard of for well-brought up young women to venture outside without hat and gloves. But what do you think their parents would have said about their ties?

READY FOR GAMES

It's easy to see from their clothes and equipment that these children have wealthy parents. The younger boy has certainly never had to wear a sailor suit handed down from either his brother or his sister, though all three of the children, you'll notice, are wearing the same style of long dark stockings.

The elder boy is dressed in a white flannel blazer and knickerbockers – a type of full knee-breech. His tie and striped cap (notice how small it is, just perching on the top of his head) are probably part of his school uniform.

The girl's smock dress, like the sailor suit, was a popular style for many years. This one is rather more elaborate than some, with its frill around the neck and over the shoulder seams.

The very shapelessness of these dresses made them immensely practical. Because they were full and didn't fit closely anywhere, they could be worn for several years before they were outgrown – provided, of course, there was a good hem to let down as the child grew. Then, when they were finally too small for one daughter, the hem could be turn-

ed up again ready for the next girl in the family – though that probably would not happen in a family like this one!

You may have noticed that the boy's tennis racket is a different shape from modern ones, but have you spotted the skirt guard on the girl's bicycle? The wires running from the mudguard to the centre of the back wheel prevent full skirts from getting caught in the spokes and causing a nasty accident – not something that is likely to happen with today's jeans or much shorter and narrower skirts.

A BEACH PICNIC

Imagine playing on the beach in clothes like these!

But it is a sign of the times that the children here are having a picnic on the beach at all. The idea that fresh air and exercise were important for a child's health was not new when this photograph was taken in 1898, but actually playing on the sand is quite different from a sedate stroll along the promenade.

However, it's not the parents who'll have to worry about getting the sand and salt out of these children's clothes. That's the job of the nannies sitting here with their small charges. (The man and woman standing up are probably the parents of one of the children, who have come to check that all is well on the beach before going about their own affairs.)

Unlike some nannies, these ones are not wearing uniform, but their dark, sensible clothes and plain little straw hats are themselves almost a uniform. Although their blouses show the influence of the fashionable 'leg of mutton' sleeves (see page 13), it would never do for a nanny, who was after all a servant, to go to such extremes of fashion – even if she could afford it.

Note that three of the women are using umbrellas as sunshades. Pale skins were still then the ideal of beauty. To the Victorians and the Edwardians, a tanned skin merely meant that you had to work out-of-doors, and so were poor. It was a long time before a tanned skin would become something to be envied.

SEWING AND DARNING

In Victorian and Edwardian times, people expected their clothes to last in a way that we'd find hard to imagine.

One reason for this was that clothes then were much more expensive in terms of a family's overall budget. Also, clothes simply weren't as readily available as they are now. The country's high streets were not full of clothes shops. Instead, there were shops selling dressmaking materials, and most people made their own clothes, or had them made if they could afford it.

For clothes to last, they had to be looked after, and any tears or worn patches mended. And, as this 1898 photograph shows, mending clothes wasn't something done only by the poor. These three young women, in blouses with the currently fashionable 'leg of mutton' sleeves, are clearly from prosperous, middle-class homes. Even so, the one in the white blouse is darning her dark cotton stockings. (Cheap, throwaway tights were over half a century in the future.)

The woman on the bench is obviously sewing, but the frayed edge of the material suggests that she's making something rather than mending it. Maybe she's doing some embroidery to set into the front of an old blouse to give it a new look.

It's not possible to see what the third woman is doing, but from the position of her hands she may be crocheting. True lacemaking (see page 20) was a difficult skill to learn, but crochet lace was relatively easy and, again, was often used to make an old dress or blouse seem new.

The women in the photograph look far more stylish than their male companion, with his portable sketching kit on his knee. His jacket fits very badly, and his trouser legs are completely shapeless. His bow-trimmed shoes, though certainly more elegant than the rest of his outfit, seem more suitable for wearing in a smart drawing room.

A BOOT FACTORY

(Above) Many of the serviceable boots seen in the photographs so far in this book were made in factories like this one, run by the Barwell Co-operative Boot and Shoe Society in Leicestershire. The lack of machines illustrates how much of the work in making boots and shoes was still done by hand – and a great deal of it by women.

Notice the full-length, sleeveless pinafores these women are wearing over their long, high-necked dresses. Such pinafores are simply longer, grown-up versions of the ones they had worn as children, and still serve the same practical purpose of keeping their dresses clean. Only much later did companies start providing overalls for their employees.

The sewing machines on the table to the left were made by the Singer Manufacturing Company, one of the pioneers of automated sewing. Their first machines were patented in 1851.

COUNTRYMAN'S SMOCK

(Right) Smocks, like the one this old man is wearing, were for many centuries the standard working garment for most countrymen. They were made of tough, generally unbleached linen or cotton, and in some parts of the country were almost a uniform. The only variations were the style of the smock and the patterns of the smocking stitches which differed slightly from region to region.

The smocking gave shape to an otherwise almost shapeless garment. Notice on this one how the smocking is used to shape and taper the full sleeves towards the wrists.

This old man and his smock have probably grown old together. His stoop and his swollen hands suggest a lifetime in the fields, at work in all weathers. Though the pace of life may have been slow – no faster than a man could walk or a horse could draw a plough – the hours were very long, and most of the heavy work still had to be done by hand.

17

CONVALESCENCE

Medical knowledge has increased so much this century that illnesses such as tuberculosis (TB), diphtheria and scarlet fever, once common and highly dangerous, have now almost disappeared.

Children from the poorer parts of industrial cities were particularly vulnerable. Bad housing combined with poor hygiene and an inadequate diet kept the children's wards full in the big city hospitals.

When the children were on the mend, they were sent to seaside convalescent homes to complete their recovery. This little group was photographed at one such home at Broadstairs in Kent in 1900 – together with what appears to be the home's mascot.

The children are all wearing hats of some kind – as you'll have realized from the photos so far, it was unusual *not* to wear some sort of headgear out of doors.

The girl standing up seems very pleased with her hat, with its large ribbon bow under her chin. She probably enjoys its prettiness, in contrast to her dark dress and pinafore, and rather heavy boots.

The boy on the left wears a stiff white collar, probably made of celluloid – an early type of man-made material (which, in a different form, was used for some of the earliest films). High collars like this frequently rubbed and could make the wearer's neck very sore if they didn't fit properly.

THE MILLINER

(Right) Dressed in her Sunday best, this young woman is posing for her picture in a photographer's studio in 1900. The pedestal on which she rests her hand is real, as is the urn on it. However, the landscape behind is just a painted backcloth, provided by the photographer to make the final photo more interesting.

This woman is lucky, for she earns her living as a milliner (someone who makes hats), and so her splendid hat probably cost her very little. Her blouse, too, is lovely, with its rows of lace down the front, and lace inserts at the wrists. Have you noticed how, in almost all the photographs so far, the women's skirts have been plain and dark, while the blouses are light and pretty?

THE MIDDAY BREAK

(Above) The bell has gone, and the mill-hands stream out for their mid-day break – a photograph taken in Aberdeen in 1905.

Although it's just a working day, the girls in the foreground look quite stylish in their berets or flat, mannish caps. The girl on the right is wearing a tie, an echo of those in the photographs on pages 13 and 16.

But the three women behind them, with their shawls around their heads, would not have looked out of place among the women gutting fish in the picture on page 11. That picture was also taken in Aberdeen, but some 12 years before this one. The skirts and shawls of these three hark back to a much older way of dressing than the clothes of their workmates in the foreground.

Work in the mills making cloth was tiring, but it wasn't as tough as working on the fish quays or in the fields. These young men and women certainly don't have the worn-out look of the crofting family on page 10. They still have the energy to laugh and smile, and to enjoy themselves.

And, on their nights out, the women will probably dress in very much the same way as the milliner in the photograph opposite.

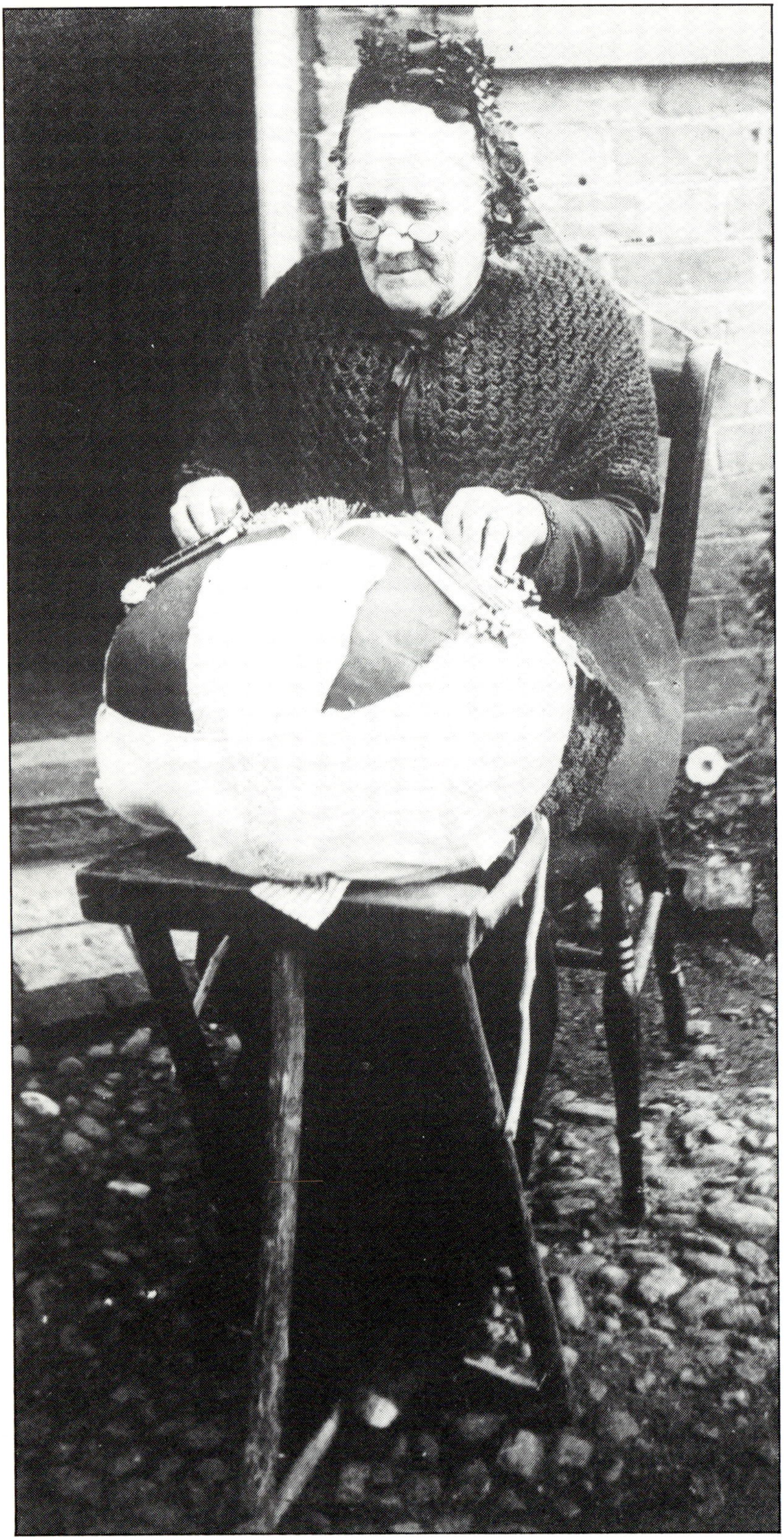

THE LACEMAKER

(Left) What a wonderful photograph this is! Although taken in 1904 the details are all very clear, from the little ribbon cap the old lacemaker is wearing on her head to the uneven stone path outside her front door.

She's making pillow-lace (worked with bobbins on a pillow), probably as she's done since she was a girl. The steel-framed spectacles on her nose also suggest years of doing fine, intricate work, often in poor light.

Down each side of her pillow hang the bobbins of thread, each bobbin ending in brightly coloured glass beads. In the centre of the pillow you can see the rows of closely packed

A CHRISTENING

pins around which the thread on the bobbins is wound. Some of the completed lace is hanging over the end of the cushion nearest the camera.

Of all the many different types of textile workers in the country, the lacemakers, even at the turn of the century, were among the most highly skilled – although much of the traditional, hand-made lace was by then being replaced by machine-made alternatives.

Perhaps some of this old lady's lace was used in the dresses and hats of the people at the magnificent christening party in the photograph above?

There can be no doubt that this christening is an important family occasion, nor that this is a group of very wealthy people. The family already seems to have two daughters; perhaps the new baby is a boy.

What a wonderful array of grand afternoon dresses! (Morning dresses would be plainer, and evening dresses even grander and more low-cut in style.)

Look at the voluminous christening robe the baby is wearing. It completely covers the mother's lap – you can see the hem of her darker dress showing below the robe's deep lace edging. It's probably a family heir-

loom, worn by the two girls at their christenings, too.

There's a tremendous amount of detail in this photograph. Notice, for example, the quite magnificent hats, and the great variety of accessories – parasols, gloves, jewellery, a tiny handbag, and ribbons and lace everywhere.

Have you spotted the distinct family likeness between the two men in top hats, and several of the women in the photograph, including the one with the parasol standing second from right? They all have the same sort of nose and mouth, and are probably related.

21

PROVIDENCE PLACE

The people and setting of this photograph make a stark contrast to the photograph on the previous page. This is Providence Place in north London, photographed in 1908.

The few gallant window-boxes do little to lift the gloom of the alley, with its central drain and graffiti on the walls. Some of the children may be grinning, but the grown-ups look as miserable and dejected as their surroundings.

The slumped shoulders of the woman in the doorway on the right are echoed by the sagging lines of her face. The right sleeve of her blouse has been torn and mended so that there's a frayed edge all round the outside. It's a sad reflection of her attitude to life that she can't see the point of mending clothes more carefully.

Washing and drying clothes in homes like these wasn't easy. Many houses didn't have even a cold tap indoors – water was drawn from the communal pump or tap at the end of the alley. From that you'll realize there was certainly no hot running water.

The only way to have hot water was to heat it in a big container on the fire or kitchen range. Clothes were scrubbed on a corrugated washboard to loosen the dirt – there were no detergents with enzymes to do that for you. To stop white clothes from getting a yellow, dingy look, a 'blue bag' (a bag containing blue powder) was added to the wash.

Alleys as narrow as this were very airless places, so drying clothes must have been a problem, especially in winter. In addition, the air was so polluted in the cities that even if the washing was clean when put out to dry, it was likely before long to be covered with soot and smuts.

MAKING DO

(Above) Life isn't easy for this woman – the clothes she and her children are wearing prove that – but home for her is clearly not somewhere like Providence Place. The chairs the children are standing on, and the trellis behind, suggest that they're in their own little garden, with chairs brought out from the house.

Even so, the children's clothes show that their mother can't afford to buy them new winter coats. No coat for a boy was ever designed with a collar and shoulder line like this one! And the roughly turned-up hem and worn appearance of the material are all too obvious.

The little girl's coat is more successful. It's a gallant attempt to recreate the coats worn by so many children from wealthier homes: made of tweed, with velvet collars and cuffs. But notice how this coat, too, was originally intended for someone larger than its present wearer – the badly fitting sleeve is the clue here.

The children's shoes, too, look as if they've had many different feet in them. But, rich or poor, their socks are as wrinkled as Virginia Grace's nearly fifty years earlier (page 7)!

BY THE SEA

To judge from clothes, this mother (or is she a grandmother?) has never known what it's like to dress herself or her daughter from bazaars and other people's cast-offs. She wears a beautifully cut tweed suit, a high-necked blouse, and a hat with a plume and face veil.

The girl's thick coat has a velvet collar and rather mannish lapels, an echo of her mother's jacket. Under it she's wearing a tartan skirt or dress – you can see the hem hanging below the coat.

Even though they're at the seaside, their clothes suggest that it's not summer – or else that it's very cold even for a British summer. Only the doll, as elegantly dressed as they are, is wearing thin clothes.

Have you spotted the dark patch on the shingle? That's probably the shadow of the photographer taking this picture.

23

WEDDING DAY

Changing fashions affect even the most traditional of occasions, and weddings are no exception.

This wedding group was photographed in a Leicestershire village in about 1910. The dresses of the bride and her two bridesmaids (if they're already married, they'll be called matrons of honour) are much closer to the ordinary styles of the day than are the 'traditional' wedding dresses worn now.

The hats are not so different from the milliner's on page 19. But if, after the wedding, the girls feel they are a little too grand for their ordinary lives, they can always be retrimmed.

Hats were still an essential part of a woman's wardrobe, whether she was rich or poor. But hats don't wear out in the same way as, for example, shoes. So, to ring the changes, most women changed the trimmings on their hats – it was much cheaper than buying a new one.

The bridegroom and best man look very smart in their Royal Artillery uniforms. Notice that they are wearing rosettes pinned to their jackets, not buttonholes, although the groom seems to have a spray of flowers tucked into his breast-pocket. But why does his jacket have fewer buttons on it than that of his best man? Notice, too, the elegant sleeve decorations.

And look at the way the third man – the bride's father perhaps – has fastened his jacket, with just the top button. It's certainly not because the jacket is too small for him. However, if you look at the photographs on page 10, you'll see that the farmer and the crofter's son have also fastened their jackets in the same way. All three are farmworkers of one kind or another, so perhaps it was the accepted way for them to fasten their jackets.

Sadly, married life did not last long for these newly-weds. In 1914 the First World War began, and the two men, as serving soldiers, would have been among the first to be sent to fight.

WAR WORK

When the First World War began in 1914, the government was faced with a dilemma. It needed as many men in the armed forces as possible, but who would do the work they left behind? And then there was all the extra work caused by the war: making ammunition and explosives, filling shells, and so on.

The answer was obvious, but revolutionary. Women.

Since the end of the last century, more and more young working-class women had been taking jobs in shops and offices. Plenty more had worked in the textile mills of northern England and Scotland (see page 19). Few, however, had ever been employed in factories, doing 'heavy'

work with machines. That state of affairs changed fast.

The enormous armies fielded by both sides in the war needed equally vast quantities of armaments and ammunition. This photograph, taken in about 1915, shows part of the assembly line in a munitions factory.

There were some practical problems to overcome when women first started working in factories. One of the most important was, what should the new workers wear? The work was too dirty for the traditional sleeveless pinafores (page 17). Generally it involved moving machinery, so long hair and full skirts and sleeves were dangerous. And, of course, women had not worn trou-

sers before. (By this time women cyclists often wore divided skirts, but the skirts were still quite full and lady-like – giving no hint of the wearer's shape beneath.)

You can see the solution to the problem in this photograph: baggy overalls with hoods to cover the hair, and face masks for those working with dusty, dangerous substances. But if this factory is anything to go by, no one has yet thought of supplying gloves to fit the women's hands!

Most of the women lost their jobs when the war ended in 1918. But they had proved they were able to work as equals alongside men, and this brought a fundamental change of attitude in society.

BEACH CLOTHES

This family scene from 1923 makes a striking contrast with the beach pictures on pages 15 and 23. The clothes here are almost modern, and certainly they are more like our own clothes than any in the photographs so far in this book.

There are some differences, of course. The boy's clothes are an example. He's wearing a knitted woollen suit – that's why the shorts look so shapeless. Wool may be warm for a cold British summer's day, but it isn't the most practical material to dry once it is wet – and it's difficult not to get wet when playing by the sea.

Few men would bother now to wear a shirt and tie on the beach (some don't ever bother with ties) but, even so, the boy's father is clearly wearing holiday clothes – white flannels and white boots. And it's interesting to note that he has no hat. He probably still wore a hat to work each day, because most people did, but perhaps he never liked it and is pleased to have the chance to leave it at home.

The photographer who took the picture has a good eye for business. Not only does he supply deckchairs for his sitters, but the chairs have his company's name painted on them, so the photograph will act as an advertisement. It's just a pity that the sitters' heads obscure the firm's full name!

ROYAL ASCOT

(Right) It's June 1923, and time once again for the fashionable racegoer to be seen at Royal Ascot. In keeping with the occasion, this elegant group are using a horse-drawn coach to get a grandstand view of the races – though it looks from the photograph as if they may be getting a good view of a marquee instead.

The men are in morning dress (in top hats and tail-coats), a tradition still observed even now at Royal Ascot. The women, too, are in their best clothes. That tradition also is still followed, though the styles of clothes regarded as 'best' have changed many times since 1923. Notice that these dresses have no waists; instead, the full tops are gathered into a wide band resting on the hips – a fashion typical of the 1920s.

Although most of the hats have wide brims, the woman wearing the white fur over her shoulders has spotted the coming trend: deep-crowned, narrow-brimmed cloches.

Now as then, Royal Ascot is still a great place to see extravagant hats.

A DAY AT HENLEY

(Above) The photographer is herself being photographed at another important social occasion: Henley Royal Regatta.

The two photographs (did hers come out as well as this one?) were taken in July 1926 – just over three years after the picture on the left. Look at the changes that have happened to women's clothes. Although the waists are still dropped, the hems are very much shorter – in fact they're about the same length as we'd wear them today. And some of the dresses even have short sleeves.

The hats are not the wide-brimmed confections worn at Ascot. Most of the brims are considerably narrower – and notice the deep crown on the hat worn by the woman with the Japanese parasol. Shoe styles seem to have little variety – just low heels, with straps across the instep.

Like Ascot, Henley has a traditional style of dress for men: a striped blazer and cap, and white flannel trousers. The stripes of the blazer and cap vary according to the wearer's rowing club – even though he may not have rowed for years.

27

DOING THE IRONING

How lucky we are to have all today's easy-care fabrics and modern domestic appliances, for this is how ironing was done before the ironing board was introduced.

The photograph above was taken on Humberside in 1927. All too clearly, it shows a poor home. The mother is using an old-fashioned flat iron to iron a toddler's nightdress. There were no thermostatic controls on irons like this. You just heated them on the fire or kitchen range until they were hot enough to iron the clothes.

Two irons were usually on the go at once: one being used and the other heating up. Here, though, for some reason, the second iron is perched on top of a large mug.

Notice how the table and the tablecloth are protected from the iron's heat by a doubled-over blanket.

A WIDOW'S WEEDS

(Right) This poor woman's husband has recently died and she is in deep mourning. By 1927, when this photograph was taken, it was more unusual for a widow to follow the Victorian practice and wear black clothes – generally known as widow's weeds.

Even mourning clothes, however, follow current fashions. This widow's clothes are very different from those worn by the two women on page 9. Notice the dress's straight bodice gathered into a hipband, the bar shoes and the deep-crowned cloche hat. Covering the hat, and hanging down the back, is a crepe veil. In Victorian times she would have worn it over her face.

She is also wearing jet mourning jewellery, but you'll notice how much lighter it is in style than the jewellery on page 9. Similarly, the length of her necklace echoes the fashion of the time.

CELEBRATION DINNER

(Above) Dressed in their best, guests at the London Welsh Society's annual St David's Day dinner pause to have their photograph taken.

By comparing these women's clothes with those on the previous three pages you'll guess – correctly – that this photograph, too, dates from the 1920s. The actual year, in fact, is 1929.

Waists are clearly still out of fashion – splendid if you didn't really have one, but sad if it was the best part of your figure. Even so, the rather shapeless dresses these four women are wearing look more natural (and certainly a lot more comfortable) than the fashions, such as those on pages 7 and 9, where the bust and waist were strongly emphasized.

Shawls seem to be the currently fashionable evening wrap, although the lady with the white fox fur is playing safe with a shawl *and* a fur.

Shoe styles, you'll notice, are becoming very slightly more varied. The heels are higher – and those on the shoes of the woman on the left are shaped as well.

Men's evening dress has changed very little. You'll see photographs of grand dinners today where the male guests are wearing exactly the same style of white ties and tails as here. What has changed, however, is that evening dress like this is now worn on many fewer occasions than it was in 1929.

WEDDING GROUP

(Right) Photographs are now an important part of the wedding ritual. This couple, with their bridesmaids, best man and families, are posing for photographs outside St Columba's Church in Walthamstow, east London, in August 1935.

Wedding clothes have changed a great deal since 1910, when the group on page 24 was photographed. These bridesmaids may be able to wear their dresses again, for a dance perhaps (unlike today, long dresses were still generally worn). But the bride probably never will: hers is a wedding dress of the sort we know today, and its distinctive style is quite different from the sort of clothes she would normally wear.

Rather than military uniform, the men here have lounge suits of a type they probably wore most days – even if these ones are new for the occasion.

A note accompanying the original photograph states that the flowers cost £8 – a tremendous amount of money in those days, even though you'd be lucky now to get a single bouquet this size for £8!

SEASIDE TRICKSTER

(Below) Whatever tricks this seaside conjuror is doing, he's clearly not impressing his audience. Look at the faces of the two men on the right – they're quite determined not to be fooled.

From their clothes, it would seem that this group are here for a day trip, dressed in their 'Sunday best'. The man on the right is particularly smart. Notice the watch-chain across the front of his waistcoat.

Despite the coats and macs, the lady's hat suggests that it's summer. It is made of straw and decorated with artificial flowers. In winter she'd wear a very similar hat, but it would be made of a warmer material, such as felt, and decorated with a ribbon and perhaps a small feather.

WINDOW-SHOPPING

(Right) Unfortunately the reflections in the glass make it difficult to see what this lady is looking at. She was photographed window-shopping in Bolton, now part of Greater Manchester, in 1938.

Is she looking at something she needs, or has she spotted a particularly pretty item and gone off into a happy dream about wearing it? She's certainly dressed quite stylishly. Her hat with its bold decoration, her fur cravat, and her bar shoes with shaped heels all suggest an interest in clothes, even though her figure is no longer quite what it used to be.

Perhaps she's comparing the prices here with those in the costumier's shop – across the still cobbled street. You can see 'ostumier' written across the shop's blind. What we would call a jacket and skirt, or a suit for women, were known for many years as 'costumes'. Even though you can't see what's in the shop, the word partly visible on the blind tells you that it sells women's clothes.

Notice that the lady is carrying a pair of gloves. These, like hats, were still an important accessory, and part of every woman's outdoor dress. In the winter, of course, gloves were and still are very practical. In summer, however, they were often just a nuisance, even though summer gloves were made only of cotton or very thin leather.

The fact that this lady isn't wearing her gloves suggests that she has them with her out of habit, rather than for any practical purpose.

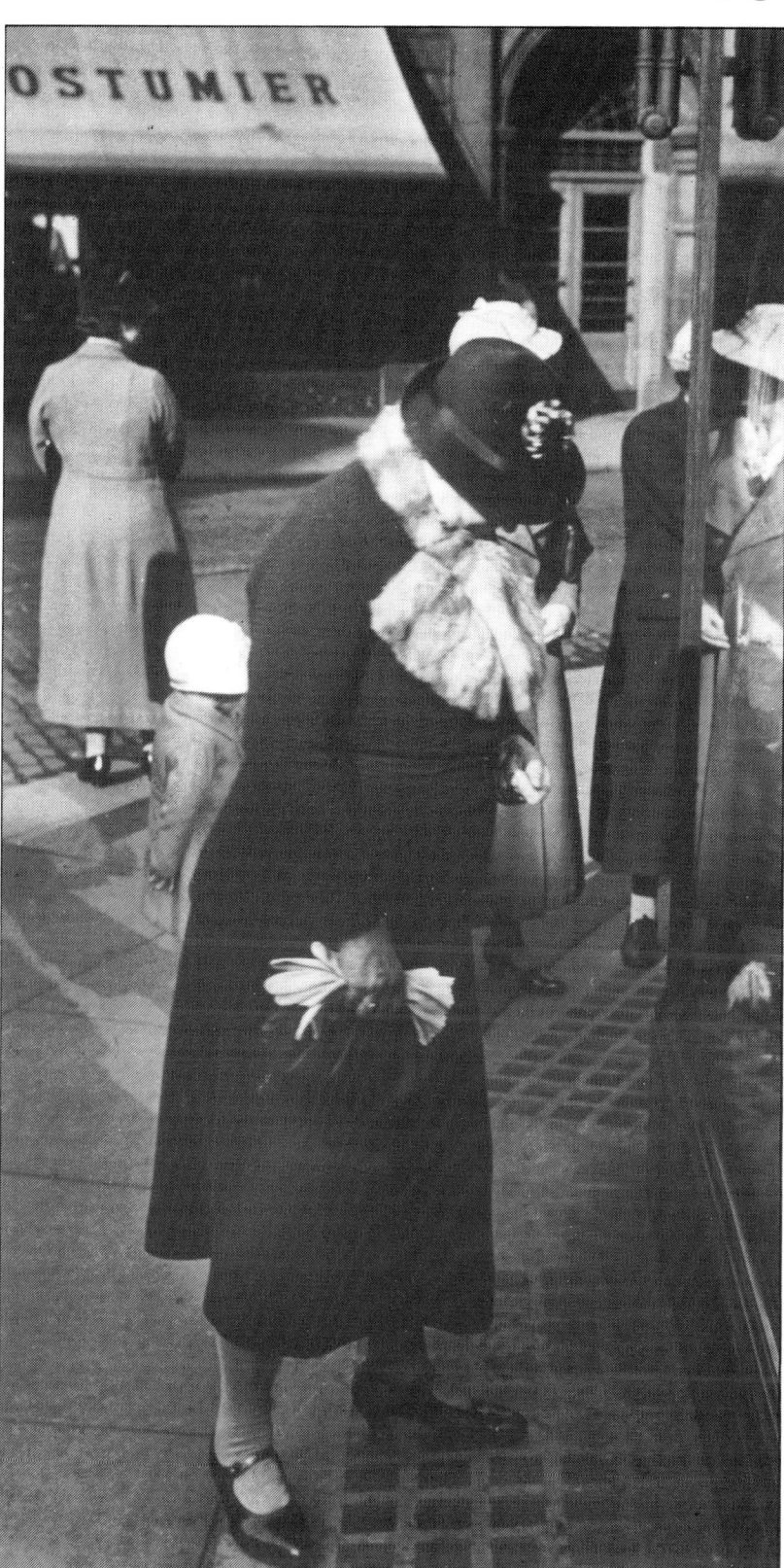

BOND STREET

(Left) Despite all the efforts of the politicians, tension in Europe, which had been growing throughout the 1930s, came to a head in 1939. As a result of the aggressive policy of Hitler's government, Britain and France declared war on Germany.

In the first few months of the war – when, in fact, nothing much happened – the British government feared that the Germans would launch a vicious aerial bombardment, with poisoned gas as well as ordinary bombs. As a result, everyone was issued with a gas mask, so that they could breathe safely when there was an attack. You took your gas masks everywhere – to work, to school, or, as here, out for a stroll along fashionable Bond Street.

Bond Street, then as now, was one of the smartest and most expensive shopping streets in London. These two women, their gas masks in the cardboard boxes slung across their shoulders, are dressed in the height of fashion.

The close-fitting line of their hip-length, waisted jackets is echoed by the slim skirts. Each skirt has a pleat to make walking easier – in the dark suit it's in the back seam, in the pale one it's in a side seam.

The shadow on the pavement shows a very clear silhouette of the woman on the right. The silhouette is topped off by a shallow crowned hat (a contrast to the cloches of the 1920s), tied at the back of the head with a striped ribbon.

Notice, too, the high-heeled, 'sling-back' shoes and the seamed stockings – tights were still worn only on stage.

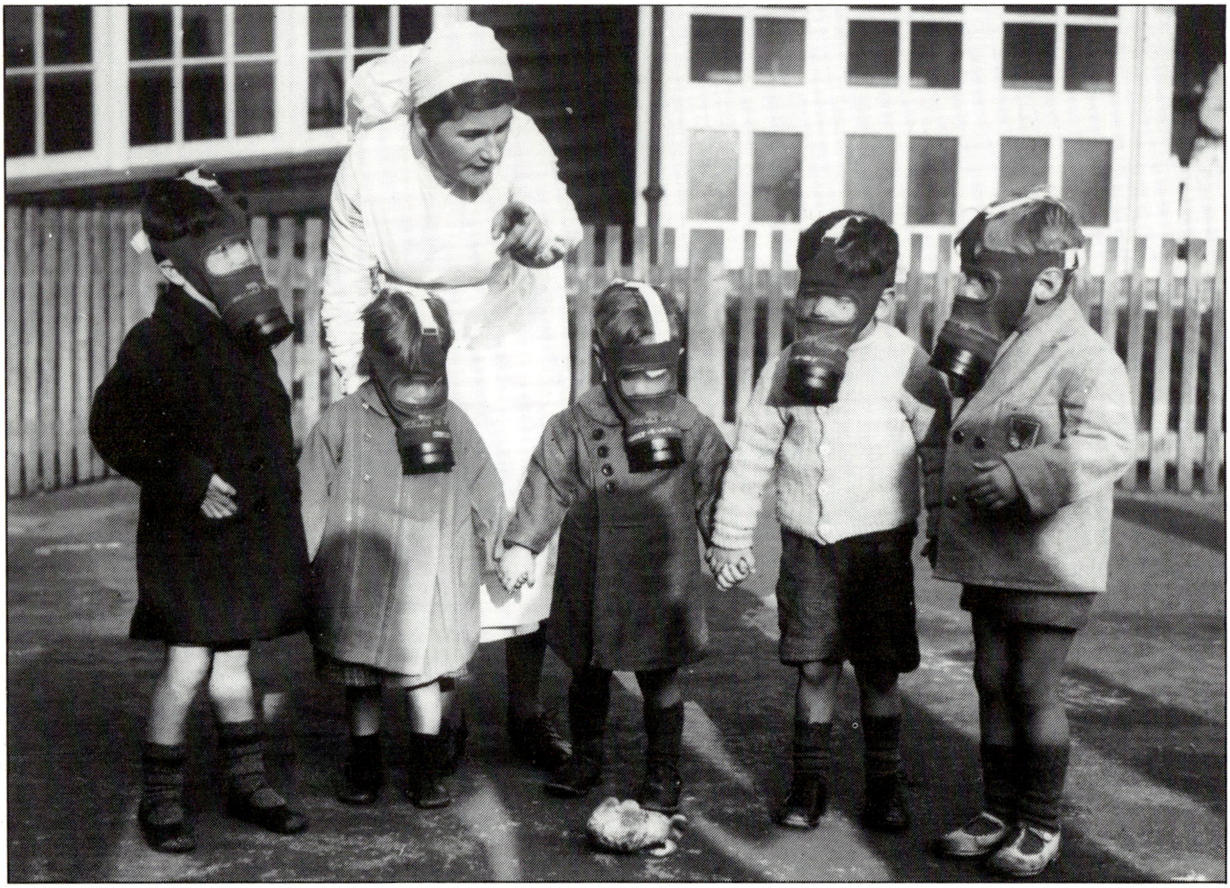

A CHILDREN'S HOME

(Left) Making sure that small children put their gas masks on properly was a nightmare, especially if you worked in a children's home like this one and had lots of children to look after.

It wasn't easy finding clothes for them, either. This rather sad, rag-tag little group wears an assortment of clothes that have been given to the home. The clothes have all seen better days and probably many different wearers, but even so they give an idea of children's clothes at the end of the 1930s. Most were still just smaller versions of what adults wore.

Notice the boy on the right, with his knitted shorts and rather smart jacket. And what's that lying on the ground in front of the children – a soft toy, perhaps?

THE HABERDASHERY

The window of Mrs Wood's haberdashery shop in Front Street, Arnold, Nottinghamshire, shows the range of goods usually carried by such shops.

There are clothes for toddlers as well as jerseys for adults, socks in many sizes, and a wide selection of knitting wool. Tea towels, table-cloths, tray cloths and place mats jostle for display space with the clothes. And, as the sign on the window above the doors shows, Mrs Wood also stocks Hercules blouses and overalls.

This photograph was taken in 1940, and Mrs Wood will find it difficult to maintain such a selection in the coming years, as the Second World War drags on. Not only will she and her customers have to cope with clothes rationing, but the government will control the styles, and the quality of the cloth.

There was no place for clothes with full or pleated skirts when materials were scarce and needed for more essential things, such as army uniforms for example. Even the number of pockets and buttons was strictly regulated.

Although the war ended in 1945, the shortages and controls lasted for several more years as Britain tried to rebuild her economy. In a phrase popular during the war, it continued to be a time of 'Make do and mend'.

STREET GAMES

Despite all the shortages, some children clearly had clever mothers, or perhaps grandmothers. The five children in fancy dress in this photograph must have been the envy of the rest of their street.

Their costumes reflect the time when this photograph was taken: the early 1940s. The little boy in the tin helmet is dressed as an ARP (Air Raid Precaution) warden. Can you spot what the other uniforms represent?

Only one of the children appears to have a gas mask – it's in the square box being dangled by one of the spectators sitting on the wall. After the first year or so of the war, when the dreaded German gas attacks did not take place, people no longer worried about taking their masks with them everywhere.

But, despite the novelty of 'uniforms' and gas masks, there's nothing new about what the children are playing. Hopscotch is a very ancient game. The squares were scratched with fingers or sticks in the dust, long before they were marked out in chalk on city pavements.

QUEUEING

(Right) The queue was a familiar sight in wartime Britain. Suddenly everything was in short supply and these women, like everyone else, found themselves having to queue for things in the shops that they had taken for granted a few years earlier.

If you wonder why there are no shop windows in this street, it's because they've been covered up with wood and corrugated iron. A bomb had probably exploded nearby, breaking all the glass.

Notice that most of the women are carrying wicker shopping baskets – colourful plastic carriers are really quite new. And though some of the women have scarves on their heads, a few continue to wear hats, showing the strength of a tradition – despite radically different, and difficult, circumstances.

It will be several years before many of the women here will be able to buy a new hat or a new winter coat. And their stockings, made out of thick knitted cotton called 'lisle', would have to be mended and darned as much as possible to make them last.

But despite the difficulties, most of the women seem cheerful, and can manage a friendly smile for the photographer.

THE NEW LOOK

(Above) This is a strange photograph. Despite the writing on the bridge, it was actually taken in 1948, *not* 1938.

What happened was that a film crew was shooting a film supposed to be taking place in London in 1938. They didn't want its accuracy spoiled by any pedestrians walking in front of the camera wearing the New Look that had come in since the end of the war.

In 1947, women's fashion underwent a dramatic change. The 'New Look', as it was immediately christened, was introduced by the great French couturier, Christian Dior.

The longer, fuller skirts and the brighter, lighter fabrics caught on instantly. It was such a welcome change from the drab styles of the war years.

Of course, not everyone could afford the complete New Look at once. This girl has teemed her new skirt with an older, rather straight jacket. Even so, it's enough for an anxious film assistant to ask her to cross the road and walk over Westminster Bridge on the other side.

He, too, appears to be fashionably dressed. Notice his slicked-down hair and patterned jacket – and his very colourful tie.

35

PLAY STREET

(Left) Where can children living in inner cities play? It's a problem that has grown as cities have grown. This photograph, taken in June 1948, shows how Bootle on Merseyside tackled the problem.

Although the boy with the football is wearing shorts, this is not because he's about to play a game. Baggy shorts like these were still the standard wear for boys of this age. (Jeans, an introduction from America, did not become accepted everyday wear for children for almost another twenty years.) Making the change to long trousers was considered a sign of growing up.

The boys' jackets are the forerunners of today's anoraks. Called windcheaters, they are one of the earliest of the more casual styles that would eventually affect the clothes worn by everyone.

And notice how the girl's hair has been carefully curled, with tongs or hair curlers, or perhaps even a 'perm', to give her the wavy look fashionable at the time.

OLD-TIME DANCING

(Left) The evening is going with a swing, as members of the local Old-Time Dance Club take to the floor in Leyton Town Hall, London, in the early 1950s.

Dresses with short full skirts and sleeveless tops seem to be the current fashion together with high, slim-heeled shoes. The strappy shoes of the dancer in the middle look very modern, although you're unlikely now to see such pointed satin shoes (probably dyed to match the colour of her dress) worn by the woman in glasses.

Dinner jackets, black bow ties and slicked-down hair seem to be the regulation style for men.

The really serious dancers of both sexes are wearing white cotton gloves – not such a bad idea if the dances are energetic or you suffer from sweaty palms.

BACKSIDE VIEW

(Above) How pleased the photographer must have been to spot this group of backsides!

The ability to 'see' photographs, often in unlikely circumstances, is the hallmark of a good photographer. Today's cameras, with their automatic focusing, shutter speeds and light levels, make it easy for anyone to produce technically good pictures, so there's no excuse for taking boring ones.

This photograph was taken at Poole in Dorset in 1950. Clothes for holidays have come a long way since 1876 (see page 8). Does your father remember having a pair of shorts like any of these? And notice the striped elasticated belts worn by two of the boys – they were fastened at the front by a buckle in the shape of a snake, and were very popular for many years.

37

A JIVE SESSION

Old-time dancing might be fine for the older generation, but certainly not for the 1950s teenager. Slowly but surely, an entirely new culture was emerging, designed expressly for people in their late teens and early twenties.

Here on Tower Hill in London, in May 1954, an open-air dance is in progress, but there's nothing old-time about it. That's probably why the girl on the left is watching the feet of the other girl so closely. The band (out of sight) is playing rock 'n' roll music and, a little uncertainly, they're trying to jive.

Two of the dancers are wearing jackets with wide shawl collars, all that remains of an item of clothing considered essential 100 years earlier. The suit, or 'costume' as it was still called, of the girl on the left is made of a textured woven material now popular again. And look at her earrings – you can find very similar ones today.

Have you noticed the dark seams on the stockings of the girl with her back to the camera? There have been attempts to revive this fashion, too, but keeping seams straight is always a problem and the fashion has never really caught on.

Although the four girls are the main focus of this photograph, there are plenty of male figures in the background. They're all wearing suits and shirts with ties. But there is a sign of styles to come – their hair is considerably longer than it would have been even five years earlier.

WINDOW DISPLAY

(Above right) What a long way window display has come since 1956. Although Lowestoft in Suffolk, where this photograph was taken, was just a small seaside town, displays like this one were typical of the time. Certainly, by our standards, the window looks crowded and the clothes unattractive – particularly the blouses on their headless, armless busts.

The Americans were the first to realize the importance of window displays to attract customers. Their ideas were introduced to Britain by Gordon Selfridge. When he opened his store in London's Oxford Street in 1909, the window displays were so revolutionary, with just a few choice items tastefully arranged, that people flocked to see them even after the store had closed for the night.

Big city stores soon followed his lead, and small shops in the provinces copied it more slowly, but by turn-of-the-century standards even this window is not crowded.

Nothing is new in clothes and fashion. With the growing interest in the 1950s, a few trend-setting shops have even started to use display models like these again.

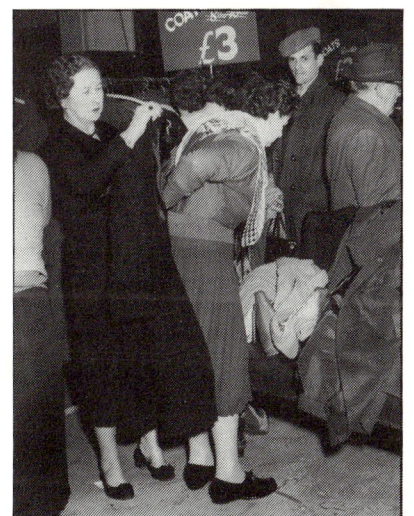

SALE TIME!

(Left) Everyone loves a bargain – a fact that the shops take full advantage of at sale time. Sales are a great way to get rid of excess stock, and all the styles the customers did not like at full price.

These coats are now only £3, although originally they sold for eight and ten guineas. (Before Britain adopted the decimal system in 1971, there were three units of currency: pounds, shillings and pence. Twelve pence equalled one shilling, twenty shillings equalled one pound. A guinea was one pound and one shilling.)

Three pounds for a warm winter coat seems an incredible bargain now, but the value of money has changed so much since then that comparisons are almost meaningless.

Notice the styles instead – they're much easier to compare! To judge by this photograph, taken in December 1957, the streets of Britain must have been very dreary in winter. Does your grandmother remember clothes like these? And what about a perm? Most of the women in the photograph have their hair cut quite short and tightly waved.

39

The two photographs here were both taken in 1960, yet they could hardly be more strongly contrasted. Between them they seem to symbolise the end of one era and the start of another.

A FASHION SHOW

(Above) Next time you walk down a busy shopping street, pause a moment and look at the way people are dressed. There will be a great variety of styles of clothes, so much so that it's hard to imagine things were ever different. But they were.

Paris had been the centre of the fashion world for nearly a century when these pictures were taken – although, ironically, it was an English designer, Charles Frederick Worth, who introduced the crinoline to France in the 1850s. (The seated ladies on page 6 are wearing crinolines.)

The influence of French fashions was enormous. It seems hard to believe now, but if the major French fashion designers (called 'couturiers') raised or lowered the hemline on their skirts, it wasn't long before most of the women in Europe were walking around with similarly shorter or longer skirts. Each season there was a fixed idea about what was or was not fashionable, and everyone tried to follow it.

Most countries had their own fashion designers, though the French were the most influential. The couturiers displayed their creations at twice yearly fashion shows, like this one in London: summer clothes in the spring, and winter clothes in the autumn.

In the audience are journalists and buyers from major stores, as well as wealthy individuals. Many of them look extremely bored.

ROCK 'N' ROLL

This photograph, taken in Birmingham in 1960, represents the start of a new era in clothes and fashion.

Today there is still a French (and British) couture industry, but it has little influence over the way most people dress. On the whole we dress now to please ourselves. There is a variety and informality about clothes

that would have been impossible to imagine even thirty years ago.

These dancers are jiving the evening away in a much more confident manner than the girls on page 38, and their informality is reflected in their clothes. Denim jeans make their first appearance in the book – though at this stage they are only for men, and are rather wider than today's slim styles.

But look at the shoes of the male dancers. Only one has a pair that are at all casual (you can see one of his feet just below the television camera). The others wear dark lace-up shoes, which suggests that they still wear much more formal clothes to work than men of their age today. And they have certainly put plenty of grease on their hair!

The women are all wearing very full skirts, ideal for twirling and twisting. And notice the girl on the right, with her black tights and white socks – that fashion has recently been revived.

1968

CARNABY STREET

The change from dressing as some outside 'authority' dictated to dressing to please yourself, did not, of course, happen overnight. Many middle-aged people, used to the relatively uniform approach, were confused about having to choose styles and colours to suit themselves, rather than following a set 'line' in clothes each season.

But for young people who either hated this approach or were too young to have known it, it was a time to experiment. However, as so often happens, in reacting against the old, they themselves adopted a new uniform – even if they were unconscious of it.

In the late 1960s, miniskirts became the female uniform. These women are lucky that they both have good legs, for the very short skirts were more unkind than most fashions to anyone with a less than perfect figure – and that means most of us!

It was summer when this photograph was taken in Carnaby Street, the fashion centre of 'Swinging London', so their bare legs and feet will get dirty but not cold.

However, with the miniskirt, tights became both popular and essential. The suspenders that were used to hold up stockings would have shown below skirts as short as these. This might have been fine in a nightclub cabaret, but not in the office, where the short skirts already raised enough eyebrows. Tights, which had originally been theatrical wear, quickly replaced stockings, at least among wearers of the mini.

Informality in dress took time to reach all sections of society. The two young men in suits may well dress in jeans and open-necked shirts at weekends, but clearly the dark two-piece suit is still an essential for success wherever they work.

FLOWER POWER

(Right) There's plenty of variety in clothing styles here: from flower children in beads and patterned shirts to a small boy in a white shirt and bow tie.

Although the presence of the flower children – peaceful protesters against what they saw as the brutality of the twentieth century – dates this photograph to the late 1960s, there are other clues showing that this is not a recent picture. Two men have ties, and at least three are wearing suits.

Look, too, at the two handbags, and compare them with the styles of bag carried today by women of the same age.

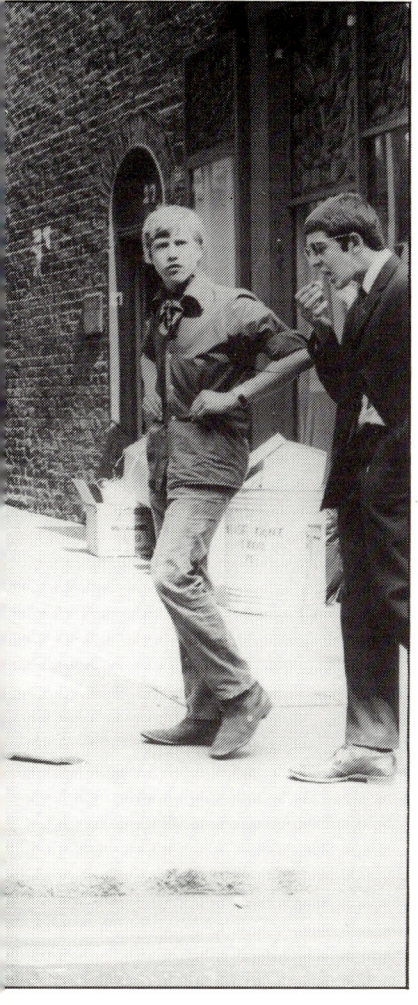

DENIMS

What a contrast between the scene above and the earlier seaside pictures. The informality of jeans and anoraks is a far cry even from the family on page 26, and beyond the wildest imaginings of the children in Wales (page 8).

But even clothes as basic as jeans and anoraks undergo subtle changes. In the 1960s, it was the done thing to shrink your jeans (often by sitting in the bath with them on), making even new ones look as pale and worn as possible, and covering them with badges – the more there were the better.

By the end of the 1970s, 'designer jeans' were the rage. The only badge on these jeans was a small label bearing the name of the designer or brand of jean. Anything else was considered very dated.

Anoraks changed too. Materials became lighter and more colourful, and the cut closer fitting. The draw-string waist and straight-from-the-shoulder style were replaced by the blouson – a fuller top fitting snugly into a waist- or hip-band.

Notice the boots of the man on the left. It isn't only women who wear higher heels – men do too!

43

PUNK FASHION

The punk look was just one of a number of teenage styles in the late 1970s and early 1980s. And not all the styles were as casual as this.

But are these 1983 punks really so casually dressed? Perhaps they seem to be, after some of the other photographs in this book. But to follow any look or style closely requires time and trouble. For example, it can take hours of dyeing, glueing and combing to produce a punk hairstyle – probably longer than it took those smart, formally dressed ladies on page 21 to get ready for the christening. What a thought!

44

1727 *Sensitivity of silver salts to light discovered*

1800 *Tom Wedgwood makes 'sun' pictures by placing leaves on specially treated leather and leaving them in the sun. The parts covered by the leaves did not darken like the rest and when they were removed their image remained on the leather*

1830 Elastic is invented

1836 William IV dies and Victoria comes to the throne

1842 Lilley & Skinner founded. Later the company became pioneers in the mass production of machine-made shoes

1849 A Frenchman, M Joly-Bellin, discovers a method of dry-cleaning clothes

1850 The magazine, *World of Fashion*, publishes dressmaking patterns

1851 The first Singer sewing machine goes on sale

1855 *Roger Fenton takes documentary photographs of the Crimean War*

1856 Thomas Burberry invents a waterproof material

1860 Worth is the first fashion designer to show his clothes on living models

1866 Pullars of Perth start a postal dry cleaning service

1873 Butterick Paper Pattern Company open a shop in Regent Street, London. The patterns are much simpler than any previously produced

1881 The Rational Dress Society is formed to make women's clothes more sensible ('rational')

1883 The Jaeger Company founded to promote the ideas and woollen underwear of Dr Gustave Jaeger

1888 *The first Kodak camera produced Kodak processing service set up by George Eastman*

1892 *Cine film is perfected*

1893 The zip fastener is patented

1894 Invention of Viyella, a mixture of cotton and wool

1895 The trouser-press invented, so making possible trouser creases and turn-ups

1901 Queen Victoria dies and Edward VII comes to the throne

1907 *Autochrome, the first practical system of colour photography, goes on sale* Rates for women shirtmakers in London is 10 old pence (about 4 new pence) per dozen finished shirts

1910 Edward VII dies and George V comes to the throne

1914 First World War begins

1918 First World War ends

1929 *Flashbulbs for cameras introduced, enabling pictures to be taken in bad light*

1935 *Kodachrome, the first modern colour film, goes on sale. In an improved version it is still used for slides*

1936 George V dies and George VI comes to the throne

1938 Discovery of nylon

1939 Second World War begins

1945 Second World War ends

1947 Christian Dior introduces the New Look *'Instant' Polaroid cameras go on sale*

1949 Clothes rationing ends

1952 George VI dies and Elizabeth II comes to the throne

1957 First Hushpuppies shoes are made

1963 *Polaroid colour cameras go on sale Kodak introduce the first 'Instamatic' cameras*

1969 *First photographs taken on the moon*

The entries in *italics* refer to developments in photography.

Things to do

FASHION PHOTOGRAPHS

Today's varied fashions make our streets interesting. If you have a camera, why not go out on a busy Saturday afternoon, and photograph as many different people and their clothes as possible.

Don't just go for the outrageous – remember that most people dress in fairly average, standard ways. The history of clothes is made up of these ordinary styles – not the fashionable (or otherwise) extremes.

Ironically, museums of costume find it easier to get grand, high-fashion clothes than ordinary every-day ones – partly because no-one thinks everyday clothes special enough for museums to want, and also partly because they are often worn out and in poor condition when finally thrown away.

If you don't have a camera, make on-the-spot sketches of the different styles of dress.

ELEGANT EXTRAS

Do you like hats or ties, fancy stockings or jolly umbrellas? Choose any accessory you particularly like and write its biography.

You'll need to find out the materials it was made of, how it was made (and cleaned), the sort of price it was sold for, who used it and on what occasions, and how it has changed from around 1850 until the present.

Some accessories, such as fans and parasols, have gone right out of fashion – perhaps you can find out why. Try to illustrate your 'biography' with pictures and sketches of your subject in all its various shapes and forms.

FASHION NOTEBOOK

What is your favourite period among those covered by this book? Choose any period that you particularly like, and perhaps whose clothes you'd like to have worn, and make a fashion notebook relating to it.

You may find fashion magazines from the 1950s and 1960s on sale in secondhand bookshops or on market stalls. Often these are very cheap, and you can cut out the illustrations and stick them in your notebook. Otherwise, make sketches of the styles and clothes of the time.

Don't forget to include both men's and women's clothes, as well as clothes for children, and clothes for a variety of occasions.

If you feel ambitious, and enjoy drawing, you could do your sketches in the rather fanciful, exaggerated style used by many fashion designers. But don't forget, someone has to be able to make clothes from the sketches!

GOING TO SCHOOL

What did children, and their teachers, wear to school? As a class project, why not trace the developments and changes in what schoolchildren wore from the 1850s until today. Don't forget, though, that few girls went to school at the beginning of this period.

Include all types of school in your survey, boarding as well as day schools, private and state schools. Remember, too, that many schools had uniforms and that these did not always reflect what children wore outside school hours. And don't forget to include the clothes worn by the teachers!

CHOOSE YOUR CLOTHES

How old are you? Try and find out as much as you can about the clothes children of your age would have worn during the period covered by this book.

Look at the Booklist for some suggestions of books to start off your research. Then select a number of years, say 1860, 1890, 1910, 1925, 1939 and 1955, and write detailed descriptions of the clothes you might have worn if you had lived then, illustrating them with drawings and paintings.

MATERIALS

Changes in materials have affected clothing styles tremendously. In 1850, when Mr and Mrs Handley were photographed (page 4), there were really very few materials from which clothes could be made. Cotton, wool, linen and silk were the main ones (although these were spun and woven in different ways to produce different effects and weights of fabric). All of them were, of course, made from natural fibres.

Now there are man-made fibres, used on their own or mixed with natural fibres. Many of the new materials came about as the result of changes in manufacturing processes. Choose two materials, one natural and one man-made, find out how they are manufactured and the clothes they are used for.

If you can obtain several small samples of the different materials, stick or staple these to your essay.

There is a tremendous number of books on clothes and fashion and the list below is just a selection. A visit to your library will undoubtedly produce other titles: from the autobiographies of famous fashion designers to histories of individual items of clothing.

Costume Reference by Marion Sichel (B.T. Batsford)
This is an excellent series of ten books. Intended to be serious works of reference, they are very well documented from contemporary sources, both textual and pictorial. It is probably easier to 'dip' into them, rather than read them from cover to cover, but even so there is a great deal of interest, and fun, to be had from them. The five titles that cover the period of this book are: *6. The Victorians*; *7. The Edwardians*; *8. 1918–1939*; *9. 1939–1950*; *10. 1950 to the present.*

English Children's Costume since 1775 by Iris Brooke and James Laver (A. & C. Black)
A much more general introduction to the subject than the *Costume Reference* series. Although the style of the book is perhaps slightly dated now, the line drawings are clear and the text (by James Laver) both informative and authoritative. The period covered by the book ends at 1920.

Handbook of English Costume in the Nineteenth Century by C.W. & P. Cunnington (Faber & Faber)
A splendidly detailed book. Illustrated throughout with contemporary illustrations, including cartoons to show what people of the time thought of the more extreme fashions. The text, describing the styles of clothes worn by all sections of society, is also largely drawn from contemporary sources and often very amusing. Again, an excellent source book.

History of Twentieth-Century Fashion by Elizabeth Ewing (B.T. Batsford)
In some ways the clothes here, being more recent, seem even funnier than those in the previous book.

Costume and Fashion by James Laver (Thames and Hudson)
A well-written and illustrated survey of an endlessly fascinating subject by an expert in the field. The book covers a much wider period, of course, than this book, but is nevertheless well worth looking at, if only for the illustrations and their captions.

A History of Children's Dress by Elizabeth Ewing (B.T. Batsford)
A general survey of a vast subject, the author nevertheless manages to make it comprehensible, as she traces the styles and trends in the way parents dressed their children over the centuries.

Shoes by June Swann (B.T. Batsford)
In books on costume and fashion the accessories often get mentioned rather as afterthoughts. This book is part of a series intended to redress the balance and treat accessories as worthwhile subjects for study in their own right. Other books in the series include: *Hats, Gloves* and *Bags and Purses*.

Shops and Shopping 1800–1914 by Alison Adburgham (Allen & Unwin)
Drawing on a wide variety of contemporary sources, this book deals with the history and development of the places where clothes were bought from the beginning of the last century to the outbreak of the First World War.

Your local museum may well have a collection devoted to clothes and fashion, and have published some booklets about the collection.

If you live in an area, such as Lancashire, which had a great cotton industry, your local library or county records office will probably have a good deal of information which will help you with the projects on the opposite page, as well as providing an interesting insight into the history of your area.

Many also have collections of old photographs which you can see on request. Even if these show only street scenes, you'll still be able to get a good idea of what people wore in their everyday lives.

Index